ALBINO ANIMALS

AA

BY KELLY MILNER HALLS

DARBY CREEK PUBLISHING

To my beautiful daughters, Kerry and Vanessa, who have grown up in an environment that celebrates diversity of every loving kind; to my amazing trio of Spokane friends who have made my life one of new hope; and lastly, to Craig Bottoms, my best childhood friend up in Friendswood, Texas, and fellow naturalist.—KMH

Published by Darby Creek Publishing,
a division of Oxford Resources, Inc.
7858 Industrial Parkway
Plain City, OH 43064
www.darbycreekpublishing.com

Cataloging-in-Publication

Halls, Kelly Milner, 1957-
Albino animals / Kelly Milner Halls.
1-58196-012-3/hardcover edition
1-58196-016-6/Scholastic Book Fairs edition
1-58196-019-0/trade softcover edition
          p. ; cm.
Summary: Everyone has probably seen the white mice or rabbits with pink eyes. Learn about these and other albino animals, the genetics that cause albinism, and the survival challenges albinos face.
1. Albinos and albinism—Juvenile literature. 2. Animal pigments—Juvenile literature. [1. Albinos and albinism. 2. Animal pigments.] I. Title.
QP670.H35 2004
572/.59 cd22
OCLC: 53209657

Text copyright © 2004 by Kelly Milner Halls
Design © 2004 by Darby Creek Publishing
Design by Keith Van Norman
Typeset in Caslon and Helvetica

Printed in the United States of America
First printing
2 4 6 8 10 9 7 5 3 1

TABLE OF CONTENTS

INTRODUCTION

I've always been fascinated by creatures of every color, shape, temperament, and size. But the sight of animals from one very special group has left me astonished and full of questions. Nearly every species on Earth has them—ruby-eyed animals with dazzling white skin, scales, feathers, or fur. They are *albinos*, animals with no pigment. *Pigment* is the coloring matter in an animal's cells or tissue. The pigment absorbs color from all the colors present in light, called the *spectrum*. A red bird has red pigment, so it absorbs red. When an animal has no pigment, it cannot absorb any color from light, so all colors are reflected off the animal, making it appear white. A lack of pigment in the eyes allows us to see the blood vessels, which makes the eyes look pink or red. But why do some animals have no pigment in the first place? It's all in the genes.

ALBINISM IN ANIMALS

Every living thing carries two copies of each *gene*, one from the mother and one from the father, each unique to its family heritage. Those genes decide characteristics, like eye color, body shape, type of hair, and height. This *genetic code* decides most of the physical attributes that make an individual unique. When both copies of the genes tell the body to produce a pigment called *melanin*, the animal will be colored like others in its breed. When both copies of the genes block the production of melanin, the animal has the traits of albinism. When one copy of the genes says "yes" to melanin (a *dominant gene*) and the other says "no," the animal will look like others within its species, but will "carry" the recessive gene to produce albino babies. A *recessive gene* is like a secret key tucked away inside its genetic code.

The following charts, called *Punnett squares*, show how the genetic code works. Think of them as a series of genetic math problems. A copy of the dominant pigment gene is represented as **A**. A copy of the recessive albino gene is represented as **a**. The dominant gene's characteristic is the one that will show up. If no dominant gene is present, then the characteristic of the recessive pair will be seen.

AA = normal pigmentation
Aa = normal pigmentation
aa = albino/no pigmentation

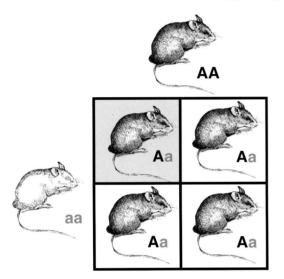

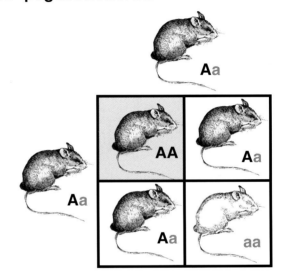

If an animal with two copies of the recessive albino gene mates with an animal with two normal copies, each of its offspring will have traditional coloring.

If both parents have one copy of the recessive gene for albinism when they mate, there is a one-in-four chance that their offspring will display albinism. Otherwise, it will have normal coloration.

Very few creatures carry the recessive gene for albinism. It is rarer yet when two carriers mate to create an albino offspring. Some animals carry a copy of the recessive gene without anyone knowing it. When that occurs, seeing the mother give birth to a pup or hatchling with albinism comes as a complete surprise. When the right combination of genetics occurs, the traits of albinism are unlocked.

Albinism can present special challenges, especially in the wild. Even so, these animals are beautiful examples of nature's diversity. Like all creatures, each one has a unique story to tell.

COLD-BLOODED SUNBATHERS

ALBINO REPTILES AND AMPHIBIANS

They lie motionless beneath a pile of crispy autumn leaves. They rest on desert rocks, soaking up morning sunshine. At night, they sing from a pond to an August moon. Some sleep underground, deep beneath the soil and a blanket of snow. They thrive on almost every continent. These are reptiles and amphibians—Earth's cold-blooded vertebrate animals.

As *cold-blooded* creatures, reptiles and amphibians depend on outside sources to warm up or cool down. This helps them keep their bodies at healthy temperatures. That's very different from warm-blooded animals, like humans. We regulate our temperatures internally by burning calories that are stored as fat.

In the water or on land, these creatures come in a variety of colors and textures. Natural *camouflage*, or protective coloring, is one of the most important tools they have in the game of survival. Green tree frogs blend in with the leaves of plants. Slithering ground snakes mimic the color of sand, stones, and soil to hide and to hunt for their food.

From day one, coloration can mean the difference between life and death. *Amphibians*—frogs, toads, and salamanders—lay their eggs in water. When those eggs hatch, the babies spend life as aquatic creatures, using their fish-like gills to draw oxygen from the water. Their colors

Albino bullfrog

reflect their watery habitats in order to keep them hidden and safe from *predation*, being eaten by hungry animals. Their colors may change as the amphibian babies mature and move on land to live using their air-breathing lungs. On land, the amphibian's coloring is just as important in keeping it alive.

Scaly-skinned and shell-covered *reptiles*—alligators, crocodiles, lizards, snakes, turtles, and tortoises—also depend on their colors to protect them. They lay clutches of leathery eggs on land. Most of the eggs hatch as miniature adults that have to fend for themselves. The exception is the alligator, whose mother often stays near the nest to care for her young. The alligator's coloration closely matches its natural surroundings, helping the animal survive and produce a new generation of the species.

Every now and then, some amphibians and reptiles are born without any colors that provide their camouflage. When this happens, they are born albino, completely lacking in any pigment. These animals are totally white and have red eyes, pink claws, and/or underparts.

Albino reptiles and amphibians have special disadvantages. Besides the usual dangers that any creature has to face in order to survive from infancy to adulthood, the lack of protective coloring of albino reptiles and amphibians makes them extra-easy targets for predators. In addition, because their skin is extremely sun-sensitive, the sun that keeps these cold-blooded animals warm can also be the cause of their deaths.

Red-eyed tree frog, typical and albino coloration

ALBINO ALLIGATORS
RARE WHITE WONDERS

Albino alligators are extremely rare. For every one hundred thousand leathery eggs that are laid, only one will hatch as an albino gator baby. According to John Brueggen, General Curator at the St. Augustine (Florida) Alligator Farm and Zoological Park, "Only about thirty albino alligators currently exist, [worldwide]."

Two of Florida's thirty resident albino reptiles are Richard (five feet, six inches long from snout to tail) and Henri (eight feet long). These white fellows look different from most alligators, but they are all gator in every other way! Their lack of pigment doesn't dull their flesh-carving teeth or their predatory instincts. "Head to head against normal alligators their size, I'd say the match would be about even," says Brueggen.

But that's not likely to happen, because Richard and Henri have their own unusual alligator habitat—and for a good reason. Unlike other gators, they live indoors. For these adult albino alligators, the sun is dangerous. An ordinary alligator spends hours basking in the sun to warm its body temperature. The dark pigment in its tough, leathery skin protects the gator from the sun's harmful ultraviolet rays. But albinos have no pigment for protection.

Albino American alligators

IT'S A BOY! IT'S A BOY! IT'S A BOY...

91°F
(34°C)
EGG INCUBATION
TEMPERATURE
FOR MALES

85°F
(30°C)
EGG INCUBATION
TEMPERATURE FOR
FEMALES

According to John Brueggen, the formula for albino alligators is simple. Breed a male albino alligator with a female albino alligator, and you'll get a clutch of up to fifty pigment-free hatchlings. So why aren't there more albino gators to gaze at? Blame it on the heat.

Zoos like the St. Augustine Alligator Farm in Florida usually get their albino babies from licensed alligator farms. And they are always boy gators. The faster a gator grows, the faster the farms can sell them to make a profit. Higher temperatures produce boy alligators. Lower temperatures produce girls. Boy alligators grow faster than girls. So, when farmers incubate the alligator eggs, they turn up the heat.

A nest of American alligator eggs

"They would burn," Brueggen says, "and they would keep burning until they blistered." Because Richard and Henri don't recognize their vulnerability, Brueggen has to take precautions on their behalf. Their alligator abode is complete with custom pools to help them cool down and with safe, artificial light to warm them.

Sunlight plays an important role in an alligator's digestion, too. After eating, alligators do what all cold-blooded reptiles must do: They find a little *radiant heat*. Gators' stomachs won't begin the natural process of digestion until they get good and warm. Once an alligator is warm enough, its brain sends a signal to its stomach to begin to break down the food. In fact, if it doesn't find a source of warmth to begin the digestive chain reaction, the food will rot in its stomach and will make the gator ill. Typical gators bask in the sun to meet their need for heat. When temperatures fall below fifty degrees for more than a day or two, an alligator will stop eating—for up to three months. Then it depends on the bit of fat stored in its tail to get by.

Once a week (and only once a week), Richard and Henri each munch on a pound or two of fresh or frozen alligator food: a thirty-six-inch, sixteen-pound rodent called a *nutria*. (Smaller gators are fed nutria burgers.) After dinner is devoured, Richard and Henri must find a source of heat, just like other alligators. "We have to give them a little heat of their own," says Brueggen. Warming grids are hidden under the stones in their habitat. Richard and Henri lie on the warm zones after they eat—and nature does the rest.

NUTRIA, ANYONE?

Imported from Argentina, massive rat-like rodents known as nutria escaped captivity and reproduced in the wilds of Louisiana. Each one ate nearly four pounds of plants a day! These super-sized rodents bred so fast and ate so much that the coastal wetlands became endangered. Legalized hunting of these creatures was the only way to save the swamps.

That is bad news for the nutria, but it's good news for alligators like Richard and Henri. Hunters sell the nutria pelts to fur traders, and they sell nutria meat, which is red meat like beef, to parks and zoos. Not a scrap goes to waste.

Solving the nutria overpopulation problem was a real puzzler for the state of Louisiana. Serving nutria steaks to alligators was only one solution. Another was to encourage people to give nutria meat a try. People? Eating giant rodents? You bet! According to a Website maintained by the Louisiana Department of Wildlife and Fisheries, nutria is a healthy, red-meat alternative to beef. "Wild nutria are fussy herbivores," according to Nutria.com, "eating only the most nutritious parts of Louisiana plants. Their healthy diet gives you one, too: high in protein and low in fat and cholesterol."

Rats: the new red meat!

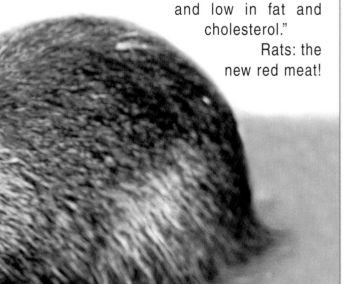

An adult nutria

S-S-SPECIAL REPTILES
ALBINO S-S-S-SNAKES

Albino snakes are as rare in the wild as albino alligators. They are also cold-blooded sunbathers, soaking up warmth whenever they can. Snake owners might think that their pets' smooth, flexible scales won't get sunburned, but Dr. Robert Sprackland, a professional *herpetologist*, a reptile scientist, and research associate at the National Museums of Scotland, says looks can be deceiving. "Albino snakes do sunburn," he says, "but not by getting red. Their bodies absorb ultraviolet light and the skin cells (*dermis*) are damaged. But by the time the snake itself senses heat, the damage may have already occurred."

Dr. Sprackland says signs of a snake's sunburn can take weeks or even months to show up. Albino snakes could get sicker and sicker without their owners realizing what is causing it. This potential skin damage makes it critical that albino snakes are protected from the harmful rays of the sun.

Apart from their special sun sensitivity, albino snakes grow and live the way any other snakes grow and live. Although they are easier for a predator to see, they are no more likely to get sick or hurt than any other snake. They grow based on what food they eat and how much of it is available. And, according to Dr. Sprackland, an albino snake can make a great pet if its owner is committed to caring for it properly. "Ask plenty of questions," he says. The animal will depend on its owner all of its life, so it is important to take that responsibility seriously.

Albino monocled cobra

ALBINO IN A HALF SHELL

Alligators can move away quickly or attack if needed. Snakes can slither away or strike a predator. But life can be risky for a slow-moving creature. An albino turtle has a lot to worry about. Albinos turtles born in the wild sometimes escape

Albino red-eared slider turtle

death. According to Larry Miller, a Kansas herpetologist, "An ornate box turtle was found near Emporia, Kansas, about twenty-five years ago, but the baby turtles are actually quite soft and face many natural predators until they are several years old." Because of this, the chance of someone finding an albino ornate box turtle is extremely rare.

Although they are as rare in the wild as other reptiles, some turtle species, like the albino red-ear turtle, are very common in pet stores, thanks to captive breeding programs. "But they tend to have poor eye sight," says Shawn Learmont of Turtle Town in Waukegan, Illinois, "and frequently need to be fed by hand." Poor vision is a common weakness among many albino animals. It can spell trouble for albino turtles whose owners release their unwanted pets back into the wild. Richard Lunsford of the Austin Turtle Page in Texas offers this warning: "If there is any risk that your turtle will ever get dumped back into the wild, do not get an albino." Unable to find its own food because of its vision problems, the animal is not likely to survive.

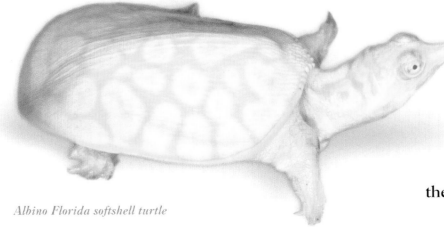

Albino Florida softshell turtle

13

"TOAD"ALLY ALBINO AMPHIBIANS
FROGS, TOAD, AND SALAMANDERS

Frogs, toads, and salamanders are amphibians. They lay their eggs in creeks, ponds, and even puddles. They will eventually grow lungs and legs so they can live on land. Their young hatch as *tadpoles*, water-bound babies that have limbless round bodies, a tail, and gills, which they use to gather oxygen.

Albinism in frogs, toads, and salamanders is more common than in some other animal species. Experts believe only one of every four hundred will be born albino. Right from the start, it is easy to tell which tadpoles will grow up to be albinos. When they emerge from their jelly-like eggs, they are not the typical dark-brown specks of wriggling life. Instead, they are almost invisible. Unlike most young albinos, their lack of coloration is actually a good thing—for a while.

Charles Drew of British Columbia, Canada, has raised many generations of albino African clawed frogs. He explains, "Being nearly transparent no doubt helps an albino tadpole blend into its

Albino toad

natural surroundings." But it's not safe for long. Within two weeks of hatching, its tiny clear body turns milky white—just as its back legs are beginning to sprout. A week later, the front legs appear. "And at five or six weeks, you have a little white frog about three-quarters of an inch long," says Drew.

Albino chaco horned frog

Once albino frogs, toads, and salamanders are mature, the road to survival becomes much more dangerous. Larry Miller of the Kansas Herpetological Society discovered dozens of tiny albino plains leopard frogs in 2001 at the Camp Creek Wetlands near Topeka, Kansas. But when he went back to the location a few months later, he found only normal frogs. Not one adult albino had survived. They couldn't hide from their natural enemies. The frogs probably sat as still as a stone, hoping the birds and snakes wouldn't see and eat them. But because their white bodies did not blend into the land-scape, they were hard for a hungry predator to miss. In the wild, this is a common fate of albino animals.

Albino crested newt

ONE WEIRD AMPHIBIAN
AN AZTEC SALAMANDER

It's a fish! It's a frog! No, it's a Mexican axolotl (axe-oh-lot-ul) salamander! Centuries ago, the ancient Aztecs discovered the strange amphibian and named it after Xolotl, the mythical god of lightning. The axolotl is native to the freshwater lakes in central Mexico.

The axolotl is closely related to the tiger salamander. Unlike most salamanders, this amphibian can be made to keep its gills for its entire lifespan, which can be fifteen years. Axolotls do not have to surface for more than a few seconds.

Melanoid albino axolotl

The thick, slippery creature is a popular pet. It is also a good research animal. "It adapts well to and thrives in laboratory conditions," says Dr. Steve Scadding of the University of Guelph in Ontario, Canada's Department of Zoology. According to Dr. Scadding, axolotls can *regenerate*, or regrow, lost limbs. Their bones can also be stained so the growth is easier to see. "There is no pigment in the albino skin," he says. "It's essentially transparent. It doesn't obscure the view of the bone."

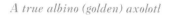

In other studies, Dr. Paul Pietsch of Indiana University uses axolotls—including Alby, an albino specimen—to learn about how eyes see and brains learn. By conducting experiments on Alby, Dr. Pietsch has made some interesting discoveries. His research

A true albino (golden) axolotl

team created a watery salamander home with half darkness and half bright, white light. When they placed Alby in a position where his body was half in the dark and half in the light, "he took a quick look around, then promptly swam into the dark half," Dr. Pietsch says. Alby stayed there even when he was offered a fat worm on the light side.

That made Dr. Pietsch wonder: Was it Alby's eyes or his skin that made him prefer the dark? Scientifically, there was only one way to find out. He removed Alby's eyes. Put in the same half-and-half environment, Alby ignored the light changes while he was blind. Removing his eyes was not as awful as it sounds. Dr. Pietsch explains that one of the amazing things about salamanders is that when their eyes are put back in, the optic nerves reconnect to the brain. In about two or three weeks, the animals can see again. After Alby's eyes were in working order, his dislike of light returned. Dr. Pietsch learned that it was Alby's eyes and not his skin that caused him to react to the light.

Dr. Pietsch's salamanders are treated humanely. "We try really hard not to hurt them," he says. "We put our animals to sleep when they are operated on and keep them under for hours so they don't wake up and thrash around."

"Alby is fine," Dr. Pietsch says. Alby still doesn't like white light, but he loves getting free laboratory worms.

WARM-BLOODED WATER WANDERERS

ALBINO SEA MAMMALS

Even before you hear the waves crashing against the shores of sand and stone, you can smell it—the moist, salty air. Unlike fish, mammals that live in water are not born with gills. As warm-blooded creatures, mammals use lungs to breathe air. They must come to the surface to breathe.

Sea lions, sea otters, and seals live both in and out of the water. They breathe just as humans do, filling their lungs with oxygen-rich air. But they can make each breath last a long time. Sea otters can go underwater without breathing for up to four minutes. Before diving, a seal takes in a series of deep breaths to flood its body with oxygen, and then actually exhales before spending as much as thirty minutes underwater. When sea mammals break the water's surface to fill their lungs with air, they inhale through their mouths and noses, just as people do.

Whales, dolphins, and porpoises live entirely in the sea, but they are mammals, too. They have one or two nostrils, called *nares* or blowholes, in the top of their heads. The blowhole allows the animal to draw air into and blow air out of its lungs. When some whales exhale through their blowhole, the force is so great that the noise can be heard almost a mile away. A sperm whale can make one deep breath last about an hour and fifteen minutes.

Sea mammals give birth to, feed, and care for their live young in or near the water. Like land animals, their coloration helps them blend in with their surroundings. Many sea mammals blend in because of *countershading.* The top part of their body is dark, while the underneath part is light. This coloration protects them when a predator looks down in the dark water, making the mammals difficult to see from above. Likewise, when a predator looks up from beneath the animal, the light underside helps the creature blend in with the lighter surface. Counter-shaded animals practically become shadows in the water. The coloration of the killer whale is a good example of counter shading. Sea mammals' coloration also helps them identify members of their own species.

Few sea mammals are born without any pigment. Rarer still are adult albino sea mammals that have somehow escaped the jaws of a predator.

Snowball, an albino porpoise at the Miami Seaquarium (1962)

SPECIAL DELIVERY
SEA LION BABY

Albino sea lion pup

As the staff biologist for the *M.S. Polaris,* Carlos Romero had seen hundreds of sea lions by the time the cruise ship headed for the Galapagos Islands in the summer of 2001. But nothing had prepared Romero for the newborn he was about to meet—and revisit for months to come.

Using a pair of powerful field glasses, Romero spotted something special. Snuggled close to her mother on a beach of dark, volcanic rock was a pale albino sea lion pup, only a few hours old. Romero took a small boat to the island, and he knew immediately what he had discovered. Romero says, "In this particular case the albinism is complete. The fur, the epidermis, and the eyes have no melanin. The pup presents a beautiful pink nose, earflaps, and flippers."

Albino sea lions are so rare that only two other cases in the wild have ever been reported. Romero was thrilled with his discovery, but, as the *Polaris* left the island in late August, he knew that he might never see the albino sea lion again. Her light coloring put the pup in extra danger. Without dark fur to help her blend in with the beach, this special sea lion would stand out as an easy target.

Three months later, to Romero's delight, a colleague named Daniel Sanchez spotted the tiny albino pup playing with the colony of dark-colored pups. Then several months passed without another sighting, and the scientists feared the worst. "Many people believed the pup had died due to its special condition," Romero explains.

WHAT DOES A SEA LION EAT? (AND WHAT EATS A SEA LION?)

Albino or not, a sea lion has to eat! An albino pup, like all other sea lions, will drink its mother's milk for one to three years. Adult sea lions eat whatever is easy to find, including anchovies, herring, rockfish, squid, and octopus. Every day an adult sea lion eats five to eight percent of its body weight—about fifteen pounds of fresh seafood. During their breeding season, sea lions eat nothing for days or weeks, so they swallow small stones to help ease their hunger.

The sea lion has to watch the deep waters where many predators are more than willing to eat a sea lion. Killer whales and great white sharks are especially dangerous. But sea lions are swift swimmers. When they sense danger, sea lions can swim as fast as twenty-five miles per hour in order to escape their enemies. Swimming in groups called *rafts* helps protect the sea lion, too.

A squid with typical coloration

But this little albino surprised the experts again when she turned up in April 2002, alive and well and growing at the same rate as a typical sea lion. The scientists reasoned that the 'missing' pup had been out in the waters, searching for food with her mother. "*Foraging* periods take months in some cases," Romero says.

Seen again in March 2003, the young sea lion was headed for her second birthday. This time Romero did a point-to-point comparison between the albino and her ordinary-colored sea lion peers—something that never had been scientifically studied before. Romero admits that his interest in the little animal is more than scientific. "It is difficult to describe the emotions I feel being able to track and witness this unusual event over a long period of time," he says. "If you are an animal lover or if you are fond of the natural world, I am pretty sure you can understand my excitement."

CANADA'S ALBINO ORCA
A SAD STORY

Bob Wright, owner of the tourist aquarium Sealand of the Pacific, had seen his share of killer whales, or *orcas*. But on March 1, 1970, as he cruised the waters off Vancouver Island in British Columbia, Canada, he had never seen anything like Chimo, a rare albino orca.

Swimming with her black-and-white podmates, Chimo stood out like a gleaming white diamond. Wright was determined to capture this gem as a mate for his male orca, Haida. A circle of boats and sailors surrounded Chimo's pod, blasting explosive devices to discourage other pods of orcas from trying to rescue their friends.

Five members of Chimo's pod were captured that day. Unfortunately, two years after her capture, Chimo was diagnosed with Chediak-higashi Syndrome—a common disorder associated with albinism. The illness caused her to have high fevers and many serious infections. She died a short time later.

It is still legal to capture orcas, but the permits are much more difficult to get than they were in 1970. It is impossible to know whether Chimo would have lived a longer life if she'd been left to her destiny at sea. Interestingly, scientists later discovered that each member of Chimo's small pod had some kind of physical distinction. Chimo was without pigment. Her mother, Scajaw, had deformities and a badly scarred lower jaw. Another orca had an odd, narrow facial structure. The scientists wondered if the pod might have been a group of outcasts—odd orcas that bonded because of their differences.

Albino orca, Chimo

A WHALE OF A TALE

Not all albino sea mammals are small. Aborigines in Australia honor a huge animal: a white humpback whale they named Migaloo, native for "white fellow." For more than ten years, Migaloo has been studied by Dr. Paul H. Forestell, a professor at Southampton College in New York and former research director for the Pacific Whale Foundation in Maui, Hawaii. Dr. Forestell keeps watch for Migaloo and continues to be amazed by its survival.

First seen by scientists in 1991, Migaloo created a sensation right away. Is Migaloo truly an albino or simply a white whale with traditional dark eyes and markings? Because it is difficult to examine the eyes and blowholes of a humpback, finding the answer is not easy. "There has never been a documented occurrence of an albino humpback whale anywhere in the world," says Forestell. "There have been a number of other species—about twenty—for which albinos have been reported, including bottlenose dolphins, pilot whales, killer whales, spinner dolphins, and sperm whales. But the occurrence is very rare."

*Albino adult
sperm whale*

Albino sperm whale calf

Even so, Dr. Forestell and others have followed the whale's movements and have documented more than fifty sightings over the years. They believe it is a true albino. "Recent photos I've seen," Forestell continues, "show some ugly bumps and swelling and cysts around the blowholes—the area of the body that must be exposed to the sun every time the animal breathes. I don't imagine the prognosis for avoiding skin cancer is all that great."

The same dangerous ultraviolet rays that make it necessary for humans to wear sunscreen can also harm albino sea mammals. Because they never leave the highly reflective waters, their risk of skin cancer is even higher. When Migaloo went unsighted between 1999 and 2003, Dr. Forestell and other whale watchers worried that cancer had claimed the young whale. Normally a humpback can live for up to ninety-five years. In July 2003, Australians rejoiced when they spotted Migaloo on the humpback's annual northern migration from frosty Antarctic oceans to warmer waters in order to mate or give birth.

According to David Paton, a researcher at the Southern Cross University Whale Research Center, Migaloo and the other humpbacks that were traveling from the frigid waters probably had not eaten for weeks. Paton says, "There is only one thing on their minds [when they migrate] and that is to go up north to find a mate or give birth." Even if Migaloo finds a partner, it is unlikely that an albino calf would be born to the pair. According to experts, the whale would have to accidentally mate with another whale that carries the recessive gene for albinism, and that is extremely rare. Even so, Migaloo is proof that "white fellows" do miraculously appear in the sea.

PINK-EYED FAVORITES

SMALL ALBINO LAND MAMMALS

They scurry, they scamper, they scratch, and they snuggle. They are small albino land mammals, common creatures that people sometimes keep as pets. Some, such as dogs and cats, are popular because they bond with humans and can be house-trained. Even tinier mammals—rats, mice, and hamsters—may not recognize their owners or show great affection, but they are easy to care for. Small albino mammals exist in the wild, too. Albino squirrels, bats, and koalas are too exotic to be pets.

Wild or tame, these little white animals aren't always happy. Small mammals are often vulnerable and easily mistreated. When these animals are abused or are irresponsibly bred, they must depend on people to rescue them. But when these special animals are treated respectfully, they can live as healthy, normal creatures.

Albino rabbit

Albino pygmy hedgehog

A PAIR OF PALE PUGS

Miss Vicki could hardly walk when she arrived at the ABRI Veterinary Hospital in Salem, North Carolina, in 2002. Kind strangers spotted the feeble dog and her canine companion, Vinnie, staggering along the side of a road. The two albino pugs had been abused and were exhausted, sick, and hungry. The medical staff at ABRI suspected uncaring puppy breeders had turned Miss Vicki and Vinnie loose simply because the dogs were too old and sick to provide them with more albino babies. Both dogs had heartworms. Vinnie was almost completely blind, and Vicki's eyesight had been preserved, but her internal organs were badly damaged.

When Lana Applegate, president of Pug Rescue of North Carolina, heard about the pair of pugs, she stepped in to help the vulnerable animals. Applegate found a loving foster home for Vinnie, where he quickly bonded with his new family and a new pug "brother." She kept Miss Vicki herself, but admitted it was heartbreaking to care for the sick pug. Heartworm treatments nearly killed Miss Vicki. "She stopped eating after the first treatment," says Applegate.

The dog likely would have starved to death if

Miss Vicki,
an albino pug

her new owner hadn't accidentally found an answer. "It was a miracle," Applegate remembers. "We opened a can of SPAM, and it all turned around. She took a few bites and eventually ate the whole can."

Once she was strong enough, Miss Vicki underwent surgery. The dog's body began to recover, but Applegate was determined to heal Miss Vicki's bruised spirit as well. The once-neglected dog learned to play and enjoy a normal dog life. "She chews on a cow hoof now," Applegate says, "and she's started playing with toys."

Miss Vicki now serves as the Goodwill Ambassador for the local Pug Rescue group. Applegate has an explanation for how Miss Vicky was able to keep her eyesight while Vinnie suffered from near blindness. "As a breeding female, Miss Vicki was probably confined to a small indoor space [without sunlight], and it saved her vision," Applegate says. Vinnie probably was turned outside when his mate was caring for her pups. "I keep her inside mostly now, too. But she has 'doggles'—vet-approved goggles—to wear when she does go outside."

Unfortunately, Miss Vicki and Vinnie's story is not unique. Some owners will purposely breed animals for albinism because a rare dog can be sold for more money than an "ordinary" dog. An irresponsible breeder will trade an animal's health for money. Miss Vicki and her owner are determined to let people know about the dangers of breeding for albinism in puppies. "Miss Vicki is a firm believer in education," Applegate says. "As the official Pug Rescue 'spokes-pug,' she wants people to understand the albino plight."

FLORIDA'S FROSTY FELINES

Most animal breeders would agree that it is best to be careful when breeding adult cats only to produce albino offspring. But Bengal cat breeder Tina Pollock of Alva, Florida, admits that the tiny white kittens with pink eyes and faint cream-colored spots are hard to resist. A Bengal cat is a relatively new feline breed that is famous for its lovely markings and its close blood relation to the rare snow leopard. These cats are intelligent and friendly and, unlike most felines, love to swim and play in water.

Tina's husband Jon gave her a pair of typically colored Bengal cats, Lady Akasha and Baby Boy, as gifts. The Pollocks decided to breed and hand-raise Bengal kittens for others who wanted these special pets. Akasha had seven kittens in March 2003, and the Pollocks were surprised when three of them were snow-white! "We call them Snow Bengals," Tina says. The Pollocks have welcomed several white kittens since then.

According to the owners, albino Bengal cats are special. "They are incredibly sweet," Tina says. The white cats can go outside, just not in direct light and not all day. Their sensitive eyes and skin can take only small doses of the bright Florida sun.

The Pollocks do not breed the cats to get albinos on purpose. "We like to be surprised," says Tina. "You see, every litter is like Christmas for us. And once in a while, we get snow."

Bengal cat, Lady Akasha, and her albino kitten

ALBINO MICE
CLOSE TO CLONES

Albino mouse

For many years, the medical community has counted on albino mice to help test the use of drugs against human diseases like cancer and high blood pressure. Mice have a genetic makeup that is similar to humans'. In other words, if a sick mouse gets well after taking a certain drug, then a person with the same sickness might get well, too.

But there was a problem. Scientists couldn't count on the same results every time a drug was tested. Mice from different families might react differently to the same drugs—just because of their genetics. So they used mice that had been bred to produce albinism. Their genetic codes were almost identical—like a huge family of nearly duplicate albino mice. No lab was complete without its copies of little white mice.

Those days are practically over now, says Dr. Vivienne Reeve, Senior Research Fellow Faculty of Veterinary Science at the University of Sydney NSW. Modern science has found a way to breed special mice for different experiments—and not just albino rodents. "More pigmented mice are used these days than albino mice," she says. "Today, many genetically altered mice are created to respond clearly to various medical needs." That means mice are bred specially for certain medical tests, not just for a lack of pigment. "Most of those mice are brown or black," Dr. Reeve admits. Now albino mice aren't the only helpers in the lab.

NUTTY FOR WHITE SQUIRRELS

Albino squirrel

Moving from the world of tame animals to the wild ones can get a little crazy. Just ask any brown or black tree-climbing squirrel, and he'll flash his bushy tail in agreement. But when a squirrel is born albino, things can get downright nuts.

A white squirrel on brown bark does not "blend in," even in Denton, Texas. But this squirrel doesn't know he's white, so he waits, unaware of how visible he really is. Sometimes called "Lucky"—in celebration of the fact that he's escaped harm—the University of North Texas's favorite squirrel frequently lounges on concrete benches near the Willis Library. When startled, he does what all squirrels do: He scampers up a tree and waits, motionless, thinking he's invisible. Little does he know that he's a campus standout.

One hundred and sixty-four members of the University of North Texas Albino Squirrel Preservation Society pay tribute to their snow-white hero with T-shirts, fundraisers, and environmental demonstrations. "It's important to us," says ASPS president T.J. Zambrono. "We care about the little guy."

Further north in Olney, Illinois, no one knows how the town's albino squirrel colony started. Some say a hunter captured an albino mating pair in 1902 and set them up for display in Jasper Bank's Saloon. A town official supposedly ordered the wild creatures to be released into the wild. The male was immediately gobbled up by a fox, but the female survived to give birth to tiny albino babies, which grew up to produce more pure-white offspring.

Today the colony still flourishes and about two hundred healthy albino squirrels exist, thanks to community and state protective legislation. Olney's law-enforcement officers have albino squirrel insignia patches on their uniforms. The Olney city clerk doubles as an albino squirrel rehabilitation expert, nursing wounded individuals back to health for re-release into the wild. Plans are in the works for an Olney Albino Squirrel Festival sometime in the future.

Some of the old-timers of nearby Marionville, Missouri, believe the white squirrels of Olney, Illinois, came from their squirrel population, kidnapped

Q&A: FIVE FURRY FRIENDS

Some tiny albino mammals make great pets. Here are a few fun facts about five snow-colored creatures.

Why does my rabbit have ruby-red eyes?
According to the Dublin Society for Prevention of Cruelty to Animals, the lack of pigment in the pupils and irises of an albino rabbit (or any true albino animal for that matter) makes it possible to see the blood vessels inside its eyes. That's what makes their eyes look so ruby red.

Is my ferret a jill or a hob?
That's a personal question. Like many other mammals, there is a special name for a female ferret— a *jill*—and a different name for a male ferret—a *hob*. These terms apply only to ferrets that have not been spayed or neutered. In that case, your girl becomes a *sprite* and your boy will be a *gib*. And a group of ferrets is called a *business*.

How do I pick a perfect prickly pet?
Albino hedgehogs are adorable, but they aren't the only prickly option. Cream, cinnamon, black, dark brown, and spotted are other preferred color choices, according to the North American Hedgehog Association.

How sweet is the life of a sugar glider?
An albino sugar glider is cute and unusual, but before you buy one as a pet, keep one thing in mind. Sugar gliders live up to fifteen years, according to Sandman Sugar Gliders in Dallas, Texas. Don't become a sugar glider owner unless you're ready for a lifetime commitment.

Does my rat need glasses?
Albino rats sometimes weave their heads from side to side, but don't worry. They don't see as well as other rats, but the motion makes it easier for them to judge distance. If you keep them in a familiar environment, they'll be just fine.

SOCCER SQUIRREL SURVIVAL

When a soccer ball sent five-week-old Persil and her nest crashing from the tree where she'd been born, she escaped with only a bloody nose. But the sight of a scarlet trickle against snow-white fur alarmed some compassionate strangers. They scooped up the tiny albino and her dark-gray brother, Daz, and delivered them to Ted Burden, founder of the London Wildcare Center in Surrey, England.

"Both were a little [injured]," Burden says, "but they have recovered very well from the trauma."

Gobbling nuts and chopped fruit (and chocolate chip cookies every now and then), they should live as long as eight years in captivity. They will remain at the Center for the rest of their days. For albino Persil, nearly every day in the Center is one more day than she would have survived on her own.

"Persil would be unlikely to [live] beyond a few weeks," Burden admits, "owing to her increased chances of being caught by dogs or cats."

Even before she had to worry about hungry predators, Persil had defied the odds—just by being born without pigment. Only one in one hundred thousand squirrels are born albino, according to Burden. Now that she's found a new, protective home at the Center, bright-eyed bushy-tailed Persil will be safe from cats, dogs, and soccer balls.

Persil, an albino squirrel baby

sometime in the nineteenth century. Others think the ancestors of Marionville's white squirrels escaped from a circus wagon. In either case, what's left of the Marionville albino squirrel colony is still doing well—and with good reason. If you try to harm an albino squirrel in Marionville, you will have to pull out your checkbook and pay one thousand dollars for endangering the rare local wildlife. (Olney fines its squirrel offenders $750.)

Marionville's experts say the majority of their squirrels are no longer albino, but rather white crossbreeds of the original albino strain and the native Eastern gray squirrel. But the rodents haven't been scientifically studied, so it's hard to say for sure. There is no doubt about the town's affection for white squirrels, though. From the "Welcome to Marionville" sign that features a friendly, waving white squirrel to the White Squirrel Hollow Bed and Breakfast Inn, Marionville is nuts about these pale creatures, from their button pink noses to their white bushy tails.

GOING BATTY

Not all small mammals are cuddly critters you can take home to show your mother. But Bat World president Amanda Lollar will always welcome bat babies in her nursery, especially if the bat is as special as pure-white Casper.

Bats are the only true flying mammals. According to Lollar, albinism happens only once in every two million bats. So, when she strolled into the Bat World safe haven in Mineral Wells, Texas, in 1998 and scooped up the four-inch-long, pink-eyed creature, she knew she was holding something truly special.

"I found him during a routine check of our wild sanctuary," Lollar says. A historic sandstone building constructed in 1899, this crumbling structure provides safe refuge for thousands of migrating bats, including five hundred nesting mothers every spring. Lollar and her co-workers collect any orphaned and injured bats they find during regular sanctuary inspections. Any bats that can be rehabilitated are eventually re-released into the wild, but bats with chronic injuries take up residence at Bat World facilities.

Lollar knew that this little white fellow was in trouble. An albino Mexican free-tailed bat, Casper was dehydrated, underweight, and unable to fly. Lollar said that the furry white bat had no obvious injury, but some undiagnosed problem kept him earthbound. Bat World became his permanent home. Such a unique individual stood out amid

Casper, an albino Mexican free-tailed bat

WHICH WHITE IS RIGHT?

Beauty is present in every living creature, so every example of coloration is "right." But how can you tell the difference between a white animal with albinism and a white animal that's simply white? According to the experts, it's in the eyes.

An albino animal has no pigment in its eyes—ever. Having no color, the irises and pupils are transparent, so we can see into the heart of the organ. Blood-rich vessels at the back of the inner eye give the appearance of pink or ruby-red coloring when, in fact, the eyes are literally clear.

So look for the reds of their eyes. Most of the time, the eyes will tell whether your white animal is just white—or if it's a much rarer albino.

Albino rabbits

the other brown-eyed, brown-furred captives, but Lollar says the other bats never seemed to notice. "They accepted him right away," she recalls.

For three years Casper delighted Bat World's staff and visitors as a healthy, happy member of the Mexican free-tailed bat community. Then, in 2001, he passed away after developing colon cancer, possibly caused by ingesting some pesticides, a common cause of death for bats the world over. "We care for over one hundred non-releasable bats with special needs," Lollar says. "But Casper was a favorite. He was very sweet. Casper was beautiful and will be sorely missed."

SENSATION IN SAN DIEGO
"GHOST BOY"

Zookeepers at the World-famous San Diego Zoo were amazed as they stared at the mother koala. In March of 1997, a tiny surprise poked its head out of eleven-year-old Banjeeri's pouch.

A tiny, hairless baby climbed up his mother's body and into her milk-providing pouch. Koalas are *marsupials*. They are born tiny and without hair. They climb from their mother's birth canal into her pouch. There they nurse on mother's milk for a few months as they continue to grow. Six months later, a snow-white koala baby emerged. "The appearance of the albino trait in our koala population was unexpected," says Curator of Mammals, Valerie Thompson.

Ghost Boy, an albino koala

Neither Banjeeri nor the baby's father—Blinky Bill, age fifteen—were known to carry the recessive albino gene. But this baby was definitely albino—the first albino koala baby ever born in captivity. Against his mother's traditional brown and gray fur, the baby's white fur and pink nose, ear, eyes, and claws made the infant look ghost-like. Zoo officials named the baby "Onya-Birri," meaning "Ghost Boy."

For almost four years, Onya-Birri thrilled zoo goers, popping his head back in his mother's pouch to nurse and later, nibbling eucalyptus leaves, the sole food of adult koalas. Sadly, in 2001 the rare koala died of an infection of the nervous system, a condition that was related to his albinism. Onya-Birri was one of the most beloved members of the San Diego Zoo's substantial koala colony, the largest outside of the animal's native Australia.

WHITE AND WOOLY

LARGE ALBINO LAND MAMMALS

Many small albino mammals are vulnerable and dependent on the kindness and good judgment of people in order to thrive—or even survive. In contrast, large albino mammals are often rugged-looking creatures. Some are even revered as mystical messengers.

Fur-covered and warm-blooded, these big beasts stride through timberlands, jungles, and pastures—meat-eaters and vegetarians alike—feeding their young with mother's milk, doing what they can to survive. Despite their size, these albino creatures are still vulnerable to nature and to man.

Our laws protect them. Legends exalt them. In some cases, entire nations honor and admire them. Often, when these great white visitors pass from the first breath of life to the stillness of death, they are remembered and sometimes preserved.

Albino white-tail deer

WHITE CLOUD
A LIVING LEGEND

Farming has been Daniel and Jean Shirek's family business since 1955. Buffalo ranching has been part of their North Dakota lifestyle since 1982 when their oldest son, Kenneth, bought a bull and two heifers. The grasslands agreed with the trio of buffalo. Buffalo ranching agreed with the Shireks. Through breeding and the purchase of new stock, the herd grew to more than one hundred. The Shireks thought they'd seen it all—until they witnessed a buffalo miracle.

On July 10, 1996, Daniel Shirek's grandson spotted what he thought was a strange white boulder in the pasture. To their delight, the Shireks discovered it was no stone. It was a snow-white, newborn buffalo calf, protectively surrounded by other members of the herd.

Young White Cloud and her mother

Friends and neighbors came regularly to see the lovely white calf, whom the Shireks named White Cloud. When she turned a year old, White Cloud was moved to the National Buffalo Museum in Jamestown, North Dakota. She still lives there today.

"It's a wonderful place for White Cloud, with the hills, native grasses and coulee," Jean Shirek says. "It makes more sense for her to be there than with us, because more people can see her and enjoy her."

White Cloud lives as normal a life as possible. In July 2000, she gave birth to her first calf, a brown buffalo named Princess Winona, the Lakota tribe's native word for "firstborn."

Many Native American tribes believe that this buffalo—and all white animals born to non-white parents—is sacred. The Lakota, Dakota, and Nakota tribes, collectively known as the Sioux, see the birth of a white calf as the fulfillment of prophecy. Chief Arvol Looking Horse, the Nineteenth Generation Keeper of the Sacred White Buffalo Calf Pipe, says the birth of white and albino animals is a warning that it is time "to unite for Peace and Harmony upon Mother Earth in order for our future generations to survive."

To these tribes and others, White Cloud is a messenger. But this special buffalo doesn't seem to know it. She ambles through the grasslands, not seeing very well due to her albinism, but living with dignity.

BEATING THE ODDS

According to the National Buffalo Museum in North Dakota, the odds of a white calf being delivered to a normally pigmented adult are roughly one in eight million. The odds of an albino buffalo being born are one in one billion. A proud, old, white bull named Big Medicine was the first documented example. Born in 1923, he lived thirty-six healthy years. His son, also a white calf, was born in 1937, but died only twelve years later. These two were the only known white buffaloes born in seventy-one years.

Then the numbers started to change. White buffalo babies started to show up more often. In nine years, between 1994 and 2003, more than fourteen calves—two of them true albinos—were born. Today's better recordkeeping may account for the sudden jump in numbers. In addition, an increased interest in buffalo breeding might explain the white buffalo boom.

A WHITE TIGER TALE

In the spring of 2003, keepers from the Mahendra Chaudhury Zoological Park in Northern India could hardly believe their eyes. Thirteen Royal Bengal tiger cubs had been born to three different tiger mothers. One cub was snow-white.

To the delight of zoo director Kuldeep Kumar, the cub's mother cared for the rare baby just as she did the other four normal-colored littermates. Kumar's relief was in response to the tigress's history. Three years earlier, she had abandoned her first white cub, Zulie. Ten days later, the tiny tiger died.

Three months after its birth, this second white cub was doing well. "It's being fed by its mother in their natural habitat," Kumar says. "The albino cub is healthy and fine."

Kumar uses the term "albino" to describe his prized white cub, but tiger expert Maxine Annabell of New Zealand is skeptical. "It's a much-misused term," she says, "and, yes, even experts misuse it. For the cat to be albino, it would have to have no pigment at all. Sometimes, pigment is only seen as ghost stripes or in the eyes, claws, or eyelashes. There are only two uncon-firmed records of albino tigers, and these date back over a century. One was almost certainly a genuine albino, right down to having pink eyes. The other, like this report, is very suspect."

Peter Dickinson agrees. The British big-cat specialist and assistant curator of the Zoological Society of Wales admits that in more than a decade of working with wild cats,

White bengal tiger cub

he's never seen or heard any convincing evidence of an albino Royal Bengal ever having been born.

Still, Annabell hopes she and Dickinson are wrong. "A true albino tiger would be so rare, it would be known worldwide on every news channel you could name," she says. "It's not one hundred percent impossible. So let's keep our fingers crossed."

Time—and science—will tell whether the cub is white or albino. As soon as it is weaned from its mother's milk, zookeepers will determine its sex and make plans for a future love match. The zoo plans to find this cub a white tiger mate from the Nandankanan Zoo in Orissa, India. Most big cat cubs born in Mahendra Chaudhury Zoological Park are neutered to prevent inbreeding. But the white cub will be an exception. It will be bred to a carefully selected white tiger from another region to keep the gene pool white, but not genetically identical. An endangered species will be fortified while a rare line of white Royal Bengal tigers is born.

WHERE HAVE ALL THE TIGERS GONE?

Endangered Royal Bengal tigers are native to India, just as grizzly bears are native to the United States. But the tiger population has dropped from forty-three hundred individuals ten years ago to only thirty-five hundred today. Some sources, including the San Diego Zoo, say fewer than twenty-five hundred are freely roaming the planet today. The marshy mangrove jungles in which they den are also dwindling, due to intrusion of humans.

Zoos like the Mahendra Chaudhury Zoological Park in Punjab and preserves like Simplipal National Park in Orissa are working to save the big cats from extinction through captive breeding programs. They are also trying to better the tigers' odds by discouraging the breeding of siblings and other close relations that has weakened the big cats.

Bengal tiger cubs, traditional and white

ALBINO 'ROO AT THE ZOO

What is eight years old, four feet tall, and snow-white but is supposed to be gray? It's Mulali, the albino eastern gray kangaroo that lives at the San Francisco Zoo. This special animal—whose name means "bone" in an Australian aboriginal language—has stolen the hearts of many animal fans, especially the zoo's employees.

Like the koala, a kangaroo is a *marsupial*. The word "marsupial" actually means "pouched animal."

Mulali, an albino eastern gray kangaroo

At about eight months old, Mulali was rejected by her mother, so human attendants were needed. Hand-raised by zookeepers, Mulali became an instant favorite. Acting as surrogate "mothers," the zookeepers fashioned a special pouch of fleece blankets to make the baby marsupial feel at home. "That's where they kept her when she was nursing," says Cindy Cameron, volunteer coordinator at the San Francisco Zoo. "And that's how she slept." It was as close to simulating a real marsupial's environment as they could get.

Mulali's albinism presented zookeepers with some challenges, even after the little *joey*, or young kangaroo, was out of the pouch. Sunburn was a concern, especially before her baby fuzz was replaced by kangaroo fur. The solution was simple: baby-safe human sunscreen. Keepers trained the little 'roo to come to them when they called her so they could apply sunscreen on her delicate nose and ears.

Mulali found love among her human friends, but what would happen when she joined her fellow kangaroos? When she was a year old, she became a part of the kangaroo troop. She's already been a mother several times over, so it's clear that they liked her, too. "She is still quite used to human contact," Cameron says. "But since joining the mob, she's also fond of her own kind."

Mulali also likes her new friend, a wallaby who came from Six Flags Marine World. Janet, an eight-year-old female Bennett's wallaby, is also an albino. Wallabies look almost exactly like kangaroos, except they are smaller, about two feet tall. They both eat alfalfa hay, vegetables, fruits, and "horse chow." This albino pair also gets plenty of cool, fresh water every day.

"They spend a lot of time 'fogging' themselves, since we sometimes have more fog than sun," Cameron says. "But they're fun to watch, even when they're just white lumps on the ground."

WALLABY 20/20

Like many albino animals, Beanie, a British wallaby, had trouble with his eyesight. But it wasn't the typical sensitivity problem that is common with albinism. It was a more severe problem: cataracts. Cataracts, or protein build-ups in the lenses of the eye, made this nine-month-old marsupial's vision cloudy. Beanie kept running into fences and other wallabies. He also became confused because he could not recognize where he was.

Only one thing could be done: cataract surgery. Vets at the Animal Health Trust (AHT) in Suffolk, England, performed the delicate surgery to remove the film that clouded Beanie's sight. "We have some of the best ophthalmologists in the country, if not Europe," says AHT spokeswoman Jane Sansom, "certainly as far as animals are concerned."

After only ninety minutes, the operation was complete. Then the wallaby needed to be hospitalized for six weeks. During the recovery time, a hand-raised baby wallaby named Geoffrey kept Beanie company. Today, Beanie is bright-eyed and healthy. He charms visitors at the zoo in Malton, North Yorkshire, England.

Albino wallaby

A REALLY BIG SNOWFLAKE

Albino gorilla *Copito de Nieve*, or Snowflake, started his life as an orphan. He was about a year old when a hunter in Equatorial Guinea found him. Sold to a *naturalist* in 1966, Snowflake found a home at the Barcelona Zoo in Spain and quickly became the pride of the city.

As the zoo's dominant male gorilla, Snowball fathered six children, including two daughters—Machi and Virunga—who lived with him in Barcelona. None were albino. Three of his grandchildren also lived at the zoo: females named Nima, Batanga, and Mayany. Snowflake played affectionately with his children and grandchildren.

Zookeepers tried to limit Snowflake's time in direct sunlight to lessen his risk to develop skin cancer. Unfortunately, he still developed the terminal condition in 2001. When three surgeries and other treatments failed to cure the aging primate, the zoo's president Jordi Portabella made a difficult decision. Snowflake's keepers would treat him with antibiotics and antidepressants to help him feel better, but they would use no painful medical

Snowflake, an albino western lowland gorilla

measures to prolong his life. Snowflake was going to be allowed to die with dignity.

The zoo's head veterinarian, Jesús Fernandez, believes this kind of cancer had not been detected in gorillas before this. The fact that Snowflake was albino, he said, might have contributed to his contracting the disease.

Resigned to the eventual loss of the beloved great ape, Portabella informed the general public in September 2003. Snowflake's many fans at the Barcelona Zoo had only a short time to say goodbye. Streams of people flocked to the zoo to pay their last respects.

On November 24, 2003, Snowflake died. He was nearly forty years old. Postcards of this rare animal can be found all over Barcelona, commemorating their beloved snow-white gorilla.

WHAT A DEER!

Like so many kinds of animals, it can be hard to tell an albino deer from a deer born with white fur. There is one way to see the real thing, though. At the Florence Wild Rivers Interpretive Center in Wisconsin, an albino buck has been preserved for all visitors to see.

Albino deer are protected in Wisconsin. It is against the law to shoot one of the rare individuals. Even so, in 1992, a hunter took down a seven-year-old whitewall buck with ruby-red eyes and pale gray hooves. The community and the game warden were so disturbed by the death of the albino deer that they decided to memorialize the 225-pound, eight-point buck. They commissioned North Star Taxidermy to stuff the beautiful animal. In November 1993, a leaping albino deer was unveiled—complete with simulated ruby-red eyes.

Two white-tail fawns, one typically colored and one albino

SPECIAL SWIMMERS

ALBINO FISH AND SHELLFISH

How important is water to life on earth? People and most other life forms drink water to quench thirst. Water is a hunting ground for food. It is a form of recreation, too, refreshing us when the weather is hot. Water in the form of seas, lakes, ponds, and rivers provides a calm setting for thinking deep thoughts. Water is all of those things for us. But for fish, shellfish, and other marine creatures, water is simply home.

Like animals in other environments, aquatic animals depend on their ability to hide from hungry predators. Shells and scales are designed to blend in with the underwater scenery. Blending in is a key to their survival.

In the saltwater of seas and oceans or in the freshwater of ponds and rivers, surprises lurk. Like ghosts in fluid darkness, albino fish, lobsters, rays, sharks, and crabs somehow defy the odds and manage to survive—and even thrive.

Albino short-tailed stingray

Albino channel catfish

RAINBOW WHITE

The words "rainbow" and "albino" seem to be opposites. But in nature, an albino rainbow trout is a real thing—and a rare creature. Normally, rainbow trout reflect the colors of their natural habitat. Minerals that color the rocks and soils of their watery regions determine the colors a rainbow trout will become. Those rocks and soils are not white, so the albino rainbow trout defies the protective coloring in nature.

"In almost thirty years I have never heard of one [just appearing] in the wild," says Thomas Pettengill, Sport Fisheries and Aquatic Education Coordinator for the State of Utah Department of Natural Resources. But during those same three decades, he's seen thousands of albinos raised in captivity, thanks to a fish hatchery in Kamas, Utah.

Hundreds of the fishery-raised, pigment-free rainbow trout were introduced into Utah's freshwater lakes and ponds for one reason: They were easy to see in the water. Often the state fish-and-game officials add to or *stock* the natural populations in many lakes and ponds. But some Utah fishermen didn't believe it was happening. "We were getting complaints that we weren't stocking

Albino brook trout

50

fish when we actually were making regular plants," Pettengill says.
"By stocking albinos, *anglers*—people
who fish—could see them, and the phone calls
and complaints went way down." Signs of approval

*Albino
rainbow
trout*

sprang up quickly. New albino-friendly activities like underwater field trips
became popular. At Mirror Lake near Orem, Utah, ordinary trout cruise through the lake,
but they are often hard to see. In the muddy Mirror Lake waters you can see the albino trout
even from a distance.

Though successful in Utah's waterways, albino rainbow trout don't always survive in
their new environments. In 2000, David Hedley introduced ten of the thirty small albino trout
at his hatchery into a pond at the Hedley Trout Farm in Ontario, Canada. Speaking of the
ten, Hedley says, "The larger [native] fish immediately turned on them. That was the end of
those."

He raised the remaining twenty albinos with regular trout their own size before releas-
ing them into the bigger ponds with the rest of his fish population. After they had grown to
be more than ten inches long, Hedley tried again. "They appeared to have been accepted by
the general trout population as equals," he says. "But they became easy prey for the great
blue heron, which in less than a year killed almost all of the remaining albinos." A lone
albino trout survived the ordeal and became the Hedley Trout Farm mascot.

Texas biology professor Dr. Donald Allen sees the albino fish as potential "research
assistants" in treating human eye disease. "I want to know how the albinos are able to avoid
severe and permanent light damage," Dr. Allen says. By studying how the albino trouts' eyes
are protected from damaging light rays, scientists may be able to learn how treat humans
with light-sensitive eye conditions.

WHITE ANGEL OF THE DEEP
AN ALBINO STINGRAY

When a dark stingray glides through the ocean, it looks something like an alien. Its muscular wings flap with grace and ease, as if it's from another world. When an albino stingray soars through the underwater currents, it looks like an angel.

Rees Jones of Pacific Hideaway Charters in New Zealand knows firsthand how real and rare these "angels" are. He has seen one himself. "It's been seen over several summers at Poor Knight's Island," Jones says. "The albino stands out from the others, which are dark gray." According to Jones, it's not unusual to see more than one hundred short-tailed rays at a time, hovering, then gliding up and down, riding the gentle currents. They come to find a mate and to breed.

At SeaWorld in Orlando, Florida, Michael Legg fed an albino stingray shrimp and fish by hand. About fifty assorted rays flourished in the public feeding tank. Legg says, "In a small area partitioned off from the tank, there were babies and smaller rays, including the albino," which really stood out from the rest.

Do these spirit-like animals still live in oceans and tanks worldwide? SeaWorld says there is no albino in its touch-tanks today. But Rees Jones's son, Gareth spotted a larger, snow-white stingray in the summer of 2003, not far from where he first spotted one six years ago. "We like to think it's the same one, grown bigger," Jones admits. "We like to think it survived."

Albino stingray

LONG LIVE LINCOLN THE LOBSTER

In 1997 on a cool, crisp fall day in Casco Bay, off the coast of Raymond, Maine, Bill Coopersmith, Jr., and his father were trapping lobsters to sell at their market, the Fisherman's Net. Suddenly something caught Bill's eye.

"When the trap broke water," Coopersmith says, "it just glowed. It almost looked like a toy." "It" was a true albino lobster.

Affectionately named Lincoln by a local children's songwriter, the rare-but-healthy *crustacean*, or shellfish, dined on cut-up crab parts in a cozy saltwater tank of his own. Market visitors were dazzled, and before long, a media circus began.

The lobster was of legal size to keep—just over a pound and one-eighth—and was approximately seven years old. Even though this was a nice-sized lobster, Coopersmith never imagined cooking it for dinner. Just the idea of steaming this special lobster "steamed" most people. But what would become of the albino lobster?

"A lot of aquariums wanted him," Coopersmith admits. "Even *Ripley's Believe It or Not* was calling. But we decided it was too cool to be kept in a tank for the rest of its life. We decided to let it go."

Four months after Lincoln sailed into Raymond, Maine, he sailed back out again. Some fifty miles into the Atlantic Ocean, the junior and senior Coopersmiths said goodbye to their once-in-a-lifetime discovery.

A traditional lobster and its albino counterpart

WINGED WHITE WONDERS

ALBINO BIRDS

▲·▲

Animals display colors in their skin, fur, hair, scales, and feathers. Among bird species, the variation of colors is remarkable. Some blend in, camouflaged by their earth-toned feathers, but others stand out as flashy, eye-catching creatures. Birds' colors come from two sources: pigments in their feathers or skin and the actual structure of the feathers. These "structural colors" occur when light is reflected off particles in the feathers. For example, the bright blues, greens, and other iridescent colors of peacock feathers are caused by special structures in the feathers, not by pigments.

Coloration plays different roles among bird species. The male is usually brighter colored than the female. His bright color attracts the female for mating purposes. The female's coloring is muted so she can blend in with her surroundings while sitting on her nest. Like some sea creatures, countershading protects many birds. Viewed from above, they blend in with the dark earth, but when viewed from below, they are difficult to see against the light sky.

According to famed biologist Edward O. Wilson, more than eleven thousand species of birds inhabit the planet. Of those species, twelve to fifteen percent are either threatened or endangered. And the albino birds, ones with no pigment, are the rarest of all. Without normal pigmentation to protect them, these birds are unlikely to survive in the wild.

A partial albino peacock

SNOWDROP
A ONE-IN-A-MILLION WONDER

Penguins are known for their black-and-white "tuxedos." The African penguin is a seven-pound, two-feet-tall bird covered in thick layers of short black feathers and white feathers. These birds don't fly—they swim the waters surrounding twenty-four islands between Namibia and Port Elizabeth, Africa. They are favorites at zoos around the world.

In the fall of 2002, a one-in-a-million chick hatched from a typical African penguin egg. It was not on the coast of southern Africa, but in captivity at the Bristol Zoo Gardens in the United Kingdom. Mystified staff members stared at the newborn bird. He wasn't the traditional dark, fuzzy penguin chick that they expected to see. This special baby was a true albino, covered in feathers of pure white, and gazing back at his gawkers through little ruby-red eyes.

Research confirmed that Snowdrop was the first albino penguin ever hatched in a zoo, but experts agree that he is even more exceptional than that. "I contacted my colleagues in South Africa to find out just how unusual Snowdrop is," says Duncan Bolton, curator of Bristol Zoo Gardens. "So far, they have tracked down only two recorded sightings of albino penguins in the wild."

Although inbreeding can increase the odds of a penguin being born with albinism, Snowdrop's medical caretaker, Sharon Redrobe, head of Veterinary Services, says that is not how

*Snowdrop, an albino
African penguin*

Snowdrop came to be. "The captive zoo penguin population is managed to prevent inbreeding," she says, "so this albino has been produced by a rare coincidence of two rare carrier animals breeding together."

For six weeks, the astonishing chick was held in careful isolation to give him a healthy, protected start in life. Then, on December 12, 2002, Snowdrop made his public début and charmed the hearts of thousands who lined up to see him.

As he grew, Snowdrop's "tuxedo" didn't look like any of the others' in his colony. This pure white wonder was the darling of the zoo. The community expressed concern when a deadly heat wave smothered Europe during the summer of 2003. "What's being done to protect our favorite penguin?" people asked. Bristol Zoo Gardens responded by unveiling their secret weapon. "Since Snowdrop is an albino," says zoo spokesperson Karen Rickards, "we have to be careful with the sun. So we have put some sprinklers—just like your regular garden sprinklers—in the seal and penguin coast."

Snowdrop, a Bristol Zoo Gardens favorite

Sharon Redrobe explains that albinos face other special hazards, too. "We will be monitoring [Snowdrop] for signs of diseases associated with albinism, such as skin and eye problems," she says. Some of the possible hazards include vision problems, cataracts, sunburn, and skin tumors. "But to date, his health checks have shown him to be fit and healthy, and it is possible he could live a long, healthy life—like his black-and-white relatives."

RARE RESCUE
A WHITE RED-TAILED HAWK

In December 1988, a father and son near Moorsville, North Carolina, walked beside a row of honeysuckle bushes. Out of nowhere—thud!—something hit at their feet. They were shocked to see a snow-white bird lying wounded on the path.

The men rushed the bird to the Huntersville sanctuary. According to Mathias Engelmann, the Carolina Raptor Center's rehabilitation coordinator, a quick examination revealed that it was an albino red-tailed hawk, starving and unable to fly. A volunteer veterinarian carefully examined and performed emergency surgery on the raptor, but was unable to fully repair the wing. "The hawk would not heal well enough to use the damaged wing, and so would never be able to fly," Engelmann says. Honeysuckle, named for the bushes from which he dropped, became a permanent resident at the Carolina Raptor Center. He has remained there for the past fifteen years.

Honeysuckle's feathers are all white, but is he a true albino? Honeysuckle's eyes are chocolate brown, not pink or red. The Carolina Raptor Center experts say that makes Honeysuckle a partial albino, having pigment-free feathers, but lacking the ruby-red eyes of a full albino. Few birds of any species are complete albinos; partial albinos are much more common.

A partial albino red-tailed harrier (hawk)

A FINE-FEATHERED SNOWMAN

A partial albino peacock

Peacocks strut around, showing off their shimmering green, blue, and gold tail feathers like princes on parade. But, like other bird species, white *peafowl*—a general term for peacocks, peahens, and chicks—are often called "albino" when they are only partial albinos. These lacy birds have no pigment in their feathers, but their eyes are dark brown or black, so they are not full albinos. That doesn't make them any less beautiful.

One gorgeous bird, Chantilly Snowman, was a champion white peacock. His magnificent tail fanned fifteen feet across, and his personality made him a favorite with New York State breeder Barry Koffler and poultry competition judges. Snowman died after living twelve normal, robust years. "No one and nothing was as beautiful as Snowman," Koffler admits. "He was the showpiece of the farm." According to Koffler, Snowman was not a true albino.

It is no surprise to Dennis M. Fett, teacher and director of the Peacock Information Center in Iowa, that Chantilly Snowman was not an albino bird. In more than thirteen years of studying and writing about peafowl, he has never seen a true albino. "Many breeders insist on calling dark-eyed white peafowl albinos, but it's inaccurate," he says. More than forty-five verified peafowl color types exist, according to the United Peafowl Association. Each color variation can be traced directly back to two breeds: the India and the Ceylon. White is one of the official peafowl color types; albino is not. Without those ruby-red eyes, Fett says, a white bird is just a white bird.

AN ANGEL OF A BIRD

Birds come in all sizes, and hummingbirds are among the smallest birds on the planet. "Hummers" are often colored an iridescent blue or green with ruby-colored throats. Imagine the surprise hummingbird observer Becky Laskody felt when she saw a flutter of white hovering at her feeder in Chapel Hill, North Carolina, on July 30, 2003. She knew white hummingbirds were unusual—only about one hundred had ever been seen. Of those one hundred, very few were true albinos. So she sent an email to Bill Hilton, Jr., the executive director of the Hilton Pond Center for Piedmont Natural History. Laskody thought this might be a bird he'd like to band.

Since June 1982, the nature center has banded 42,881 North Carolina hummingbirds for scientific purposes. Each tiny bird is gently caught and banded by placing a tiny, numbered aluminum band on one leg. Banding birds allows the U.S. Fish and Wildlife Service to better understand the hummingbirds' migration patterns, their growth, and their survival rates. Bill Hilton is one of only fifty hummingbird banders who is permitted by the USFWS to help carry out the important work.

Within a month, he and fellow bander, Susan Campbell, of the North Carolina Museum of Natural Sciences, were working with Laskody to band the white ruby-throated hummingbird. They were also eager to determine if it was a white hummer—or a true albino. First, Hilton and Campbell set up their remote control trap. Only twenty minutes later, they struck white gold. The tiny hummingbird, nicknamed "Angel" by the Laskody family, fluttered near the trap for a drink of

Angel, a true albino hummingbird

sugary nectar. She couldn't find her way into the trap, so she flew away. Two hours later, Angel returned and easily slipped into the cage. Hilton pushed the remote control, the cage door softly closed, and a small crowd that had gathered to watch the teamwork softly cheered.

Susan Campbell holds Angel before release

"As interesting as this bird was on the wing," Hilton says, "it was even more incredible up-close where we could see white plumage that almost glowed—plus a bright-red eye and a bill that was an indescribable, sensuous blend of orange and pink."

The bird's weight, 4.1 grams, and size confirmed that Angel was a very young female. Hilton and Campbell took plenty of pictures, banded her right leg with the number Y14536—a number no other bird will ever carry—gathered a few other important details and measurements, and then gave the bird a reassuring drink before they released her.

Hilton noticed a remarkable feature about the hummingbird. "The skin on the toes was completely transparent, and we could actually see the bird's blood vessels," he says. "The long claws were also transparent—so much so that we could observe the blood-rich area at the base of the claw that allows it to grow."

Bill Hilton is pleased to have had the chance to study the rare albino hummingbird, but he wants people to remember that banders capture birds for science, not for fun. "For the most part, humans have no business capturing healthy wild animals," he says. "We can seldom provide conditions that meet their needs. I have no problem with [experts] temporarily 'borrowing' an animal from the wild for educational purposes."

THE RAREST OF THE RARE

ALBINO INSECTS AND PLANTS

▲ ▲ ▲

Albino sulphur butterfly

You may never get to see an albino bug. According to Texas A&M University entomologist Dr. John A. Jackman, "Albinism is not a favorable trait for the survival of insects. They stand out and are quickly eaten by predators." That makes Japan's albino locust special.

Japanese research scientist Dr. Seiji Tanaka, fellow scientist Dr. Paul Pener from Israel, and others have been studying the locust, a grasshopper-like bug, at the Institute of Insect and Animal Sciences in Tsukuba, Japan. They are trying to find out what causes locusts to turn a dark brownish-black color when they crowd together in large groups and gobble up farmers' crops. A natural strain of albino locusts—or "hoppers" as the scientists call them—is helping to solve that mystery. Dr. Tanaka and his

Various locusts, including an albino specimen (bottom)

63

associates have been able to identify the hormones that tell the locusts' bodies to change color. "We found that a hormone induces various dark colors in locusts," Dr. Tanaka says, "and that the albino strain does not have this hormone."

Knowing which hormones trigger color changes might help us understand and control the changes in hopper behaviors as well. After all, if hormones change mild-mannered locusts into crop killers, blocking hormones could block the destruction, saving farmers millions of dollars.

Besides the locusts, other albino insects probably exist, too, but survival in the wild is unlikely for many reasons. "Whitish individuals are so obvious against the natural backgrounds that they get eaten by predators," Dr. Tanaka says. "And some insects find mates by using visual cues. In such cases, the lack of pigments must be a serious problem." Color is much more than an insect fashion statement. It is also a key to the insect's survival.

WHITE ROACHES

Like all insects, cockroaches don't have skeletons inside their bodies. They have protective exoskeletons that act like armor to keep their inner bodies safe. Roaches grow, but their exoskeletons don't. At least seven times between hatching and adulthood, roaches shed their outer shells. Beneath the exoskeleton is a milky-white insect. Within a few hours, its new, bigger exoskeleton will form and the white roach will be dark brown again. A white roach is not an albino—it's just temporarily "unclothed."

A white cockroach—not an albino

NO GREEN TO BE SEEN
ALBINO PLANTS

We know that animals carry the genes that create albinism, but do plants? According to expert John Zasada of the University of Alaska's Fairbanks Institute of Northern Forestry, they do—but with a lethal twist. Zasada explains that albino seedlings sprout because of the recessive genes in their parent plants, just as albino babies do in the animal kingdom. Albino *seedlings*, the "infant" form of plants, have been found among Alaskan white spruce, aspen, birch, and balsam poplar trees. A few other examples have been seen as *saplings*, new growth that is still connected to its parent by a joined root system.

Animals with albinism lack pigment, but their bodies still function almost normally. Not so in plants with albinism. Because the pigment missing in plants is *chlorophyll*, a chemical that helps plants manufacture their nutrients, plant albinism is deadly. Because they have no chlorophyll, these colorless plants are unable to change sunlight into the energy they need to grow. Seedlings seldom live more than a few days. Saplings, or root suckers, can survive longer, but only because their parent plants provide some food.

Albino plants do not live long, but you can still spot one easily enough. "To find albino plants," Zasada says, "look for those with white or pinkish leaves and stems."

An albino orchid plant

65

FROM THE AUTHOR

I grew up enchanted by pink-eyed mice and other animals with albinism. The beauty of these bright-white creatures made me curious about animal coloration. We humans are always curious about things that look "different." Curiosity is a good thing—it makes us want to learn—and the more we learn, the better we understand our world.

As I researched the information for this book, I remembered a time, not so long ago, when I strolled through the Denver Zoo with my two daughters. We spread out our picnic basket on a grassy hill and watched the world go by as we gobbled up our lunch. In the distance, I saw a group of elementary school children, probably on a summer-camp fieldtrip. All but one of the kids appeared to be African-American. As the children made their way down the sidewalk, I noticed that people began to stare at the one child who wasn't "black." I wondered why this other child drew so much attention. Then I made the connection: The special child was also African-American, but without the skin or hair pigment of her classmates. This lovely child had the traits of human albinism. She was a laughing, vibrant child, in most ways, exactly like her companions.

As I set out to research this book about albino animals, I couldn't help but think of that little girl and her "specialness." I found an organization that understands (and has helped me understand) albinism in humans. NOAH, the National Organization for Albinism and Hypopigmentation, is a volunteer organization for persons and families involved with the condition of albinism. NOAH provides information about albinism and community support for those interested in this condition.

According to NOAH, albinism is a group of inherited conditions that are caused by certain genes. These genes do not allow for the production of the pigment melanin. In all humans and animals, melanin determines the color of eyes, skin, hair, and nails, as well as the natural defenses that go with that pigment. Children born with albinism have parents who both carry the genes for albinism.

There are two categories of albinism in human beings. *Oculocutaneous albinism* (AHK-you-low-CU-tain-ee-us), or OCA, is the condition in which melanin pigment is missing in the skin, the hair, and the eyes of the individual affected. *Ocular albinism* (AHK-you-lahr), or OA, is present when melanin pigment is missing mainly in the eyes, but the skin and hair are not entirely affected. OCA is more common than OA. Most people are familiar with animals that have the traits of albinism. These animals almost always have red or pink eyes, due to the lack of pigment in the retina. But, according to NOAH, eye color in humans with albinism can vary from red to violet to blue.

One in seventeen thousand humans is born with albinism. In total, about eighteen thousand people with albinism live in the United States today. The lack of pigment makes these individuals vulnerable to certain skin conditions and vision challenges. Otherwise, people with the traits of albinism enjoy the full spectrum of human experience.

Twenty-one-year-old Bianca Knowlton hosts a website about human albinism

GLOSSARY

albinism a genetic condition that blocks the production of pigment called melanin that determines the color of skin, eyes, nails, beaks, feathers, and hair.

amphibian a cold-blooded vertebrate that spends some time on land but must breed and develop into an adult in water. Frogs, toads, newts, and salamanders are amphibians.

angler a person who fishes.

axolotl an amphibious salamander (also known as the tiger salamander) named for an Aztec god.

camouflage natural coloration or other devices used by animals to blend into their environment in order to avoid being seen by predators or prey.

cataract a clouding of the lens of the eye that blocks the passage of light.

chlorophyll the normally green pigment found in plants.

clutch the number of eggs hatched by a bird at one time; all of the birds hatched together from one clutch of eggs.

cold-blooded having a body temperature that varies based on the temperature of one's surroundings.

coulee a ravine or ditch in the landscape, often cut by a stream that has run dry.

countershading a protective color pattern of animals that helps them blend in with light and dark.

crustacean a group of arthropods (many aquatic) with exoskeletons, antennae, and often claws. Includes lobsters, shrimp, and crabs.

dermis the sensitive inner layer of skin where blood vessels are found.

digestion the process of converting food into usable energy for the body.

digits a finger, toe, or similar body part of a vertebrate.

dominant gene the controlling gene that determines a characteristic, such as eye color.

epidermis the thin, protective outer layer on the surface of an animal that protects the sensitive dermis.

exoskeleton the hard protective outer structure of an insect, spider, or crustacean.

foraging searching for food.

gene a part of DNA that contains information needed to process a characteristic, such as eye color, height, or type of hair. Genes are dominant or recessive.

genetic code the chemical code that is the basis of heredity.

habitat the place or type of place where a plant or animal naturally or normally lives or grows.

herpetologist a person who specializes in the study of reptiles and amphibians.

incubate to sit on or warm eggs in order for them to hatch.

joey a juvenile kangaroo.

krill small living things such as tiny shrimp and larvae that make up plankton and form a major food for whales.

leucism a genetic condition that looks like albinism but is not. Pigment is not absent, but is reduced, making the animal's coloration very pale.

mammal any of a class of warm-blooded vertebrates that nourish their young with milk produced in the mother's body and that have hair- or fur-covered skin.

marsupial a mammal that has a pouch in the abdomen of the female where the young are carried and fed mother's milk.

melanin a dark brown or black pigment that is responsible for coloration in skin, hair, eyes, fur, or feathers.

migration the act of moving from one region or climate to another usually on a regular schedule for purposes of breeding and/or feeding.

molars teeth with rounded or flattened surfaces, used for grinding food.

nares the openings of the nose in a vertebrate.

naturalist a person who studies plants and animals as they live in nature.

nutria a water-dwelling rodent, originally from South America, that has webbed feet and mammary glands on its back.

ocular albinism the genetic condition in which melanin (pigment) is missing in the eyes, but the hair and skin are not affected.

oculocutaneous albinism the genetic condition in which melanin (pigment) is missing in the eyes, hair, and skin.

ophthalmologist a doctor who specializes in the science that deals with the structure, function, and diseases of the eye.

orca also known as a killer whale; a black-and-white whale that inhabits the colder seas.

peafowl pheasants from Asia that have a long, brightly colored tail that can be raised and spread; commonly known as peacocks (male) and peahens (female).

pigment a natural substance in animals and plants that makes color in skin, hair, eyes, nails, and feathers.

pinnipeds any sea-dwelling mammal such as a walrus, sea lion, or seal that has a streamlined body and four flippers and eats fish and other meat.

pod a small group of marine animals, such as whales, dolphins, and seals.

predation the act hunting or preying upon animals for food.

prognosis the prospect of recovery of an individual who has a disease.

Punnett square a chart used by scientists to predict genetic traits in animals.

radiant heat heat that originates within a source and moves outward to warm the surrounding area.

raft group or gathering of seals or sea lions.

recessive gene a gene that is masked or not expressed when a dominant gene is present.

regenerate to generate or produce again a lost or damaged body part.

reptile any or a group of air-breathing vertebrates that usually lay eggs and have skin covered with scales or bony plates, such as snakes, lizards, turtles, and alligators.

sanctuary a place that provides shelter or protection.

sapling a young tree.

seedling a young plant grown from a seed.

spectrum the group of different colors including red, orange, yellow, green, blue, indigo, and violet arranged in the order of their wavelengths.

stock to get or acquire for a purpose, as in adding fish to a pond.

tadpole the larva of a frog, toad, or salamander that has a rounded body and a long tail, breathes with gills, and lives in water.

warm-blooded able to maintain a body temperature that is not dependent on the temperature of the surroundings.

BIBLIOGRAPHY

INTERVIEWS

December 2003
Campbell, Susan. Research associate, NC Museum of
  Natural Sciences, Raleigh, North Carolina.
Pollock, Tina. Bengal cat breeder, Alva, Florida.

October 2003
Hilton, Bill, Jr. Owner/bird bander, York, South Carolina.

September 2003
Jackman, Dr. John A. Professor and Extension
  Entomologist, Texas A&M University, College
  Station, Texas.
Pietsch, Dr. Paul. Department of Psychology, Indiana
  University, Bloomington, Indiana.
Suiter, Dr. Daniel R. Department of Entomology,
  University of Georgia, Athens, Georgia.

August 2003
Allen, Dr. Donald M. Trout research scientist,
  Odessa, Texas.
Cameron, Cindy. Public relations, San Francisco Zoo,
  San Francisco, California.
Coopersmith, Bill, Jr. Lobster fisherman, Raymond,
  Maine.
Dunkle, Sidney W. Biologist/teacher, Collin County
  Community College, Decatur, Georgia.
Fett, Dennis M. Director, Peacock Information Center,
  Minden, Iowa.
Galindo, Yadira. Public relations, San Diego Zoo, San
  Diego, California.
Hedley, David. Owner of Hedley Trout Farm,
  Ontario, Canada.
Martin, R. Aidan. Marine biologist, Vancouver,
  British Columbia, Canada.
Martin, Rick. Editor, *Local Fisherman News*,
  Portland, Oregon.
Pener, Dr. M. P. Hebrew University of Jerusalem, Israel.
Pettengill, Thomas. Sport Fisheries and Aquatic
  Education Coordinator, State of Utah Department of
  Natural Resources, Salt Lake City, Utah.

Tanaka, Dr. Seiji. Institute of Insect and Animal
  Sciences, Tsukuba, Japan.
Turtle, John. Fisherman, Newlyn, United Kingdom.

July 2003
Annabell, Maxine. Amateur tiger expert, Auckland,
  New Zealand.
Applegate, Lana. President Pug Rescue of
  North Carolina, Summerfield, North Carolina.
Drew, Charles. Frog breeder, Burlington, Ontario,
  Canada.
Learmont, Shawn. Turtle Town, Waukegan, Illinois.
Leggman, Michael. Freelance photographer,
  Elgin, Illinois.
Lollar, Amanda. President of Bat World, Mineral
  Wells, Texas.
Miller, Larry L. Herpetologist, Wakarusa, Kansas.
Parker, Mary Lynn. Tiger Haven, a rescue facility,
  Kingston, Tennessee.
Reeve, Dr. Vivienne. Senior Research Fellow and
Faculty of Veterinary Science, University of Sydney
  NSW, Australia.
Scadding, Dr. Steven. Department of Zoology,
  University of Guelph, Guelph, Ontario, Canada.
Sprackland, Dr. Robert. Veteranarian and Petsmart
  consultant, curator of the Virtual Museum of
  Natural History.
Zambrono, T. J. President of Albino Squirrel Preservation
  Society, Denton, Texas.

June 2003
Brueggen, John. General Curator, St. Augustine Alligator
  Farm and Zoological Park, St. Augustine, Florida.
Danikas, Captain Nick. Owner of Cape Anne Whale
  Watch, Gloucester, Massachusetts.
Forestell, Dr. Paul H. Pacific Whale Foundation, Maui,
  Hawaii.
Jones, Rees. Owner of Pacific Hideaway Charters,
  Kensington Whangarei, New Zealand.
Koffler, Barry. Poultry breeder, Hudson Valley,
  New York.

NEWSPAPERS, MAGAZINES, AND OTHER MEDIA

"Albino basks in limelight." *News Interactive.* August 2003.

"Albino Dungeness crab shows up in trap." *Local Fisherman News.* March 2002.

"American legend is made flesh." *Houston Chronicle.* September 24, 1994.

"An albino koala adds color to San Diego Zoo." *CNN Report.* June 5, 1998.

Armand, Jennifer B. and Rosemary James. "Louisiana's Amazing White Alligators." *Louisiana Environmentalist.* January/February 1994.

Billings, Dr. Alistair W. "Divers film rare albino shark in Galapagos." *Cyber Diver News Network.* January 26, 2002.

Bradford, Keri. "In Search of Frogs." *The Topeka Capital-Journal.* Featuring Larry Miller, Kansas Herpetological Society. July 20, 2001.

Burden, Ted. "Persil the albino squirrel." *BBC Southern Counties Extra.* June 2, 2003.

Crosby, Tim. "Soft Spot for White Squirrels." *American Profile.* November 11, 2001.

DeConto, Jesse J. "Albino Lobster? Only way to find out for sure is to cook it." *Portsmouth Herald.* New Hampshire. September 1, 2001.

Drew, Charles. "Albino African Clawed Frogs: The Curse of a Thousand Frogs." *Monthly Bulletin of the Hamilton and District Aquarium Society.* May 1999.

"Fate of Migaloo remains a mystery." *Courier Mail.* Queensland, Australia. September 2001.

Feris, Melanie-Ann. "No Dying Dignity." *The Star.* South Africa. September 19, 2003.

Higgitt, Duncan. "Colwyn's camels find it cool down at the zoo." *The Western Mail, IC Wales Report.* August 6, 2003.

Hoste, Bruno, and Stephen J. Simpson, Arnold DeLoof, Michael Breuer. "Behavioural differences in Locusta migratoria associated with albinism." *Physiological Entomology.* March 2003.

Looking Horse, Chief Arvol. "White buffalo teachings: a bison returns." *Star Tribune.* North Dakota. October 5, 2002.

Nash, Elizabeth. "Barcelona bids farewell to its dying albino gorilla." *The Independent.* September 16, 2003.

"Rare albino shark landed at Newlyn." *MarineConnection.org.* London, England. May 21, 2002.

"Rare whale calf in Port Elizabeth." *Dispatch (UK).* September 30, 2000.

"Rare whale lives life of mystery." *Honolulu Advertiser.* March 11, 2001.

"Snowdrop one in a million." *BBC News.* December 13, 2002.

"Spain prepare farewell to albino gorilla." *Animal Planet (AP Reports).* September 16, 2003.

Sprackland, Dr. Robert. "Ten Things You Should Know About Pet Snakes." www.petsmart.com.

Stietzer, Stephanie. "Sand Tiger Shark Dies." *Cincinnati Enquirer.* June 19, 2002.

Tanaka, Seiji, et. al. "Identification of the Gregarization-associated dark-pigmentotropin in locust through an albino mutant." *PNAS Journal.* June 8, 1999.

"Tennessee town celebrates white squirrels." *KnoxNews.com.* Kenton, Tennessee. July 6, 2003.

"Up close and personal with Migaloo." *ABC Tropical North TV* website. July 25, 2003.

"Up close and personal with Migaloo." *ABC Tropical North TV* website. July 25, 2003.

"White wallaby's woes." *BBC News/SciTech.* July 10, 2001.

Zasada, John. "Albino Plants." Article #433. Geophysical Institute, University of Alaska Fairbanks: Institute of Northern Forestry, University of Alaska.

BOOKS

Berenbaum. *Bugs in the System.* City: Helix Books, 1995.

Landau, Elaine. *Living with Albinism.* City: Franklin Watts, Inc., 1998.

Wilson, Edward O. *The Diversity of Life.* City: W. W. Norton and Company, 1999.

WEBSITES

Introduction
www.geocities.com/cfontheweb/ALBINISM.HTML
www.albinism.org/

Reptiles and Amphibians
www.uoguelph.ca/zoology/devobio/210labs/axolotl.html
www.caudata.org/axolotl/index.html
www.indiana.edu/~pietsch/behavior.html
www.nutria.com

Sea Mammals
www.dolphins.org/Learn/lmm-mant.html
www.seaotters.org/Otters/index.cfm?DocID=8
www.kidsplanet.org/factsheets/humpback_whale.html
www.expert.cc.purdue.edu/~wettlaul/chimo.html
www.der.expeditions.com
www.tmmc.org/learning/education/pinnipeds/stellarsea.asp

www.orcacentral.com/Ambassador_Nootka_Story.html
www.migaloo.org/
www.orcacentral.com/Ambassador_Chimo_Facts.html

Small Land Mammals
www.omegabbs.com/users/garth/squirrel.html
www.whitesquirrels.ca/
www.roadsideamerica.com/attract/WIMADsquirrel.html
www.tnwildside.com/stories.asp?Story=30

Large Land Mammals
www.lairweb.org.nz/tiger/albinos.html
www.thetruthseeker.co.uk/article.asp?ID=61
www.homestead.com/WhiteBuffaloMiracle/
www.bigskybuffalo.com/mystical.html
www.doubleebuffaloranch.com/
www.geocities.com/Heartland/9330/White_Lightning/
    white_lightning.html

Fish and Shellfish
www.utpb.edu/artsci/faculty/allen_d.HTM
www.state.me.us/dmr/rm/lobster/lobster.html
www.mitigationcommission.gov/hatchery/hatchery_
    kamas.html
www.mariscofish.com/
www.nationalaquarium.co.uk/
www.newportaquarium.com/
www.portsidebythebay.com/
www.sharktrust.org/cgi/main.asp?newsfirst=27
www.waterquality.utah.gov/watersheds/lakes/mirror
www.utahdiving.com/mirror.html
www.ananova.com/news/story/sm_593075.html?menu=

Birds
www.raynauds.demon.co.uk/whats-new.html#Snowdrop
www.bristolzoo.org.uk/news/121202.html
www.birdsofprey.org/
www.hiltonpond.org/
www.sites.state.pa.us/PA_Exec/PGC/w_notes/hawks.html
www.peafowl.org/

The Rarest of the Rare
www.alliancenm.com/cockroaches.html
www.maff.go.jp/mud/411.html
www.nps.gov/mora/notes/vol5-6c.html
www.bio.umass.edu/biology/kunkel/bgmolt.html

From the Author
www.cbc.umn.edu/iac/
www.nichcy.org/
www.rickguidotti.com/index.html
www.cbc.umn.edu/iac/facts.htm#problems
www.knowlton.clara.net/family/Albinism/bianca.htm

PHOTO CREDITS